William Brinton

On the selection of lives for assurance

William Brinton

On the selection of lives for assurance

ISBN/EAN: 9783337276911

Printed in Europe, USA, Canada, Australia, Japan

Cover: Foto ©Andreas Hilbeck / pixelio.de

More available books at **www.hansebooks.com**

ON THE

MEDICAL SELECTION

OF

LIVES FOR ASSURANCE.

BY

WILLIAM BRINTON, M.D.,

FELLOW OF THE ROYAL COLLEGE OF PHYSICIANS; PHYSICIAN TO ST. THOMAS'S HOSPITAL; AND
LECTURER ON PHYSIOLOGY IN THAT INSTITUTION.

Third Edition.

LONDON:
CHARLES AND EDWIN LAYTON, 150, FLEET STREET.
MDCCCLXI.

TO

RICHARD BAGGALLAY, ESQ.,

TREASURER OF ST. THOMAS'S HOSPITAL,

THESE PAGES,

THE SUBSTANCE OF A LECTURE DELIVERED IN THAT INSTITUTION,

ARE RESPECTFULLY DEDICATED,

WITH THE GRATITUDE AND ESTEEM OF

THE AUTHOR.

ADVERTISEMENT TO THE THIRD EDITION.

The Second Edition of this Pamphlet having been, for some time, exhausted, and the Author's engagements preventing him making any large or material additions to it, the Publishers have obtained his sanction for its republication in this form.

PREFACE.

THE Lecture of which the following pages are substantially a transcript was introduced by me into the Course of Forensic Medicine at St. Thomas's Hospital, in order to supply my Class with some information, which it seemed strictly in accordance with the spirit (if not the letter) of my duty to impart.

I have been induced to publish it, in the belief that such information may be useful to others than those to whom it was first addressed.

In preparing it for the press, I have made so few changes in either the matter or arrangement of the original Lecture, that I must warn the reader against anticipating more than such a short discourse might fairly be expected to afford. The brevity with which I had to treat of my subject forbade anything like full information, accurate description, or close and connected reasoning. The previous studies of my audience rendered it unnecessary for me to do more than allude to the various physiological and pathological details, by which alone my propositions could be sustained or illustrated. My purpose obliged me to state all the rules I could suggest in such a short and simple form as would allow them to be easily remembered. And lastly, though feeling bound to utter all I knew, I was naturally anxious to avoid dogmatizing on a subject in which our calculations rest on what is at present but an imperfect basis.

But though my remarks scarcely exceed the value of suggestions, I venture to hope that they are not without traces of more care than the form in which I have thought it advisable to put them together might seem to imply. At any rate, I trust that, as the summary of a large experience, communicated without much reserve, they may fulfil my chief object: namely, that of furnishing some practical hints, which may assist those members of the profession who are new to such duties, in the medical selection of Lives for Assurance.

WILLIAM BRINTON.

20, Brook Street, Grosvenor Square,
March 8th, 1856.

ON THE MEDICAL SELECTION

OF

LIVES FOR ASSURANCE.

I SHALL not occupy much of your time, Gentlemen, in discussing the strictly medico-legal bearings of Life Assurance. Many of these are indeed sufficiently obvious to spare us the necessity of any special notice. For example, since the calculations on which the theory of Life Assurance is founded, assume the natural death of healthy persons, the contract which a Policy of Assurance really forms may evidently be rendered void by the fraudulent concealment, at the time of effecting it, of some disease calculated to shorten life; or, what is equally fraudulent, by an unnatural, voluntary, and self-inflicted death. Hence a medical witness has been asked whether a person whose life was assured was the subject of any particular disease at a given time; whether, if so, the fact must have been known to the person assuring; or finally, whether the ensuing death of the assured was the result of some disease thus concealed, or of accident, or suicide, or temporary insanity.

Here, however, although it is the circumstance of an assurance having been effected which raises the questions that our evidence is required to aid in answering, still this fact no way affects the questions themselves, further than by referring their decision to a civil, instead of a criminal, court. Hence there is no need for me to repeat what it is my duty to say in other parts of this Course of Lectures upon these topics.

But I venture to devote this Lecture to a subject which, though not falling within the precise limits of FORENSIC MEDICINE, is yet so near to them, and so important for you to have some information about, as quite to deserve a longer consideration than the single hour which is all we can concede to it. I allude to the general or ordinary duties of the medical practitioner with respect to Life Assurance; and especially to *the medical examination of persons desirous of assuring their lives.*

It is probable that there is scarcely one of you present who will not hereafter be from time to time appealed to, for the purpose of instituting such examinations and reporting their results. Upon your report it will therefore often depend whether the future widow and orphan shall be provided for, or whether the overworked brain of the toiling father of a family must be further worn by anxiety for those nearest and dearest to him, the very commonest necessaries of whose existence seem to depend on the continuance of his own life. On the other hand, your decisions may seriously affect the prosperity of any Office that honours you with its confidence. In short, it would be difficult to specify any department of your future practice, the possession of skill in which will prove more useful to the public, and therefore more honourable to yourselves.

I am aware that there are some excellent authorities on the subject of Life Assurance generally, who appear to form a very low estimate of the value of medical examinations. "There can be no doubt," say they, "that could we take one thousand of the persons passing along a crowded thoroughfare at any given moment, and effect assurances on their lives, the proceeding would commercially be a sound one :—in other words, the accumulated annual premiums paid by such persons, according to our existing Life-tables, would amply cover all the payments of policies rendered necessary by their deaths. It is equally certain that some very prosperous Offices have systematically insured Lives without subjecting them to any special medical inquiry."

Bear with me, Gentlemen, for one moment, while I point out the fallacies involved in such statements ;—fallacies which I am the more anxious to expose, since they might otherwise lead you to think that I have exaggerated the importance of these duties; and therefore that less care, less skill, or a less stringent mode of examination, may hereafter enable you to discharge them.

As regards the first of these two statements, we will not lay much stress on the fact that active movement in a crowded thoroughfare is itself no bad test of tolerable health, and is therefore a tacit argument for a better one, if such can be found. Nor will we be so invidious as to expatiate on the dangerous facility of reasoning from the preterpluperfect of the subjunctive ; and collecting imaginary profits from Lives of which we can only say that they might, could, would, or should have been assured.

For, in point of fact, the real value of medical examinations is such that we might concede the full truth of this general statement, without at all narrowing the *locus standi* of our profession in relation to Life Assurance. We constitute, so to speak, the police of Life Assurance; and hence our usefulness (like that of the blue-coated guardians of our peace) must in fairness be judged of, not only by what we detect, but by what we prevent. Now there can be no question that many of the deadliest maladies to which the human frame is liable would often remain concealed to the eye of the unskilled laity, long after they could be easily detected by ordinary professional scrutiny. And since the greater his danger of death, the more important and obvious are those advantages which any individual can gain by the assurance of his life, we may feel pretty sure that, but for the careful medical scrutiny which is generally made use of, the fraudulent concealment of disease would be so frequent, that the present system of Life Assurance would be almost impossible;—in short, that, far from having that average of healthy and diseased Lives which doubtless must in theory remunerate an Office, we should really have a class of Lives far below the average; a class which would include many that might almost be regarded as selected by themselves expressly for their badness, and which would be certain in the long run to impoverish and ruin the wealthiest Assurance society.*

The second of these statements barely deserves a casual remark. In most, if not all, of the Offices which have been supposed to forego a special medical inquiry, the Board of Directors has included one or more members of our profession,

* The kindness of an eminent consulting Actuary has lately afforded me the opportunity of testing the truth of the above conjecture, by inspecting the details of a number of assurances which had been effected without any medical examination. From three or four pages of these cases— which really seemed to be a fair representation of the whole—I collected no less than forty instances of death by pulmonary consumption, at periods which averaged eighteen weeks from the date of effecting the policy, but often did not exceed three, four, or five weeks. The average loss to the society on these forty policies was exactly forty times the premiums paid. Now there are few fatal diseases which have so marked symptoms and so chronic a course as phthisis; indeed, under medical attendance of ordinary skill, I suspect its average duration is scarcely less than eighteen to twenty-four months. But the same specimen of four pages also afforded me four deaths, certified as due to natural decay, the subjects of which had attained an average of 67 years, and had been assured on an average but twenty-two weeks before thus dying of old age!

an interview with whom may therefore be regarded as constituting what is to all intents and purposes a medical examination.

Hence, although the question "Why Lives for assurance require to be selected from that average, upon the deaths of which all the calculations of the actuary are based?"—although this question, I say, is not for us to discuss, still we have seen that the most cursory answer to it well illustrates our professional duties. "It is probable that unless Lives were selected, they would not reach that average."

In like manner we may point out, that since, by the medical selection of Lives, we exclude the diseased or more dangerous cases, we thus form a healthier or less dangerous class; and therefore, that the Lives so chosen enjoy considerably more than the average of longevity. Now this excess of longevity over and above the calculated average must necessarily form an important element in what is the only reasonable guarantee for the stability of any Office;—namely, the acquisition of constant (if moderate) profits.

In passing on to consider the duties for which it is my express object to prepare you, let me first say a word or two about the peculiarities of the examination which you will have to institute, when referred to by any Office for your opinion of the value of a given Life.

In some instances it will perhaps be one of your own patients who is the subject of this inquiry. And I need scarcely say how valuable, or rather how indispensable, is the information which the habitual medical attendant of an assurer can often thus afford to an Office; and how useful an opinion you may found upon it, provided you take proper care to avoid that bias which even the most upright man may unconsciously possess towards the interests of a friend and patient. Let me remind you, however, that these circumstances altogether change your ordinary relations to him; that the mere fact of your being retained by an Office puts you into a position where you may have to become almost his antagonist: makes you a kind of " advocatus diaboli," to detect and display his every physical infirmity; and, if need be, a judge to pronounce sentence against his claims.

Frequently, however, the object of your scrutiny may be an utter stranger. And in such a case, I think it will be advisable for you to bear in mind, how widely an examination of this kind differs from the ordinary interview of a physician with his patient. Unlike the latter, the Candidate for Assurance has no reason for feeling any confidence in your skill, and knows that you are retained by the Office expressly to sift his pretensions. Far from being always and necessarily desirous of acquainting you with any flaws that he may suspect in his health, he will sometimes attempt to conceal them from your notice. And you must not wonder if he occasionally appears to wince under a searching question, or even seems disposed to resent it. In justice to him, Gentlemen, you will remember that in bringing into light his hidden physical ailments and imperfections, you are attacking some of the strongest passions and feelings of our nature. Personal vanity, love of money, love of live, and the higher and more unselfish anxieties of a husband and father—all of these must be sometimes attacked and wounded by the information you are so determined to elicit. And remembering this, though you cannot abate one jot of the stringency of your examination, you will be very careful to conduct it not only with tact, but (what is far better) with genuine kindness. You will let your scrutiny be not only thorough, but gentle and unobtrusive. And lastly, I will not insult you by dilating on the confidential nature of the information you thus acquire or by recommending you the strictest secresy with respect to it. For this is a character which you are aware it only shares with all the communications that you will have to receive in your professional capacity.

The information you have to obtain as the basis of your opinion is of three different kinds. 1. The present state of health of the person before you. 2. His past history in the same respect. 3. The peculiarities of his family.

It is not very important under which of these three heads yon commence your inquiry. But it is as well to have some definite rule, such as may aid the memory when you do not merely fill up the answers to a set of questions in a printed formula. And for some reasons it is most convenient to reverse the above natural order, and begin with the family history. A nervous person finds it less agitating to speak of others than of himself: and you, while listening to his answers respecting his relatives, can quietly scan his countenance, perhaps single out points for special examination in the subsequent part of your inquiry, or judge from his manner how far he is likely to answer more personal and important questions with candour and frankness.

Family History.—Mere longevity of ancestors is not unimportant: especially where (as is often the case) it appears to be scarcely explained by the circumstances in which life has been passed. And conversely, it is a suspicious fact to find that the various members of a family have all been cut off at a comparatively early age: even though the diseases that form the immediate cause of death are unlikely, from their nature or variety, to have been the result of any definite tendency to this or that complaint on the part of the family. The term *old age*, always a relative one, often appears to have a meaning specific to different families. Of course, the gravity of the suspicion suggested by the early deaths of a given family will vary with the number of cases on which it is founded; with the proximity of relationship (for example, is most important in the direct ancestors, especially in the father and mother); and with the nature of the fatal maladies (being on the whole most serious where these belong to the category of diseases of old age*).

The more specific reasons for this part of the inquiry are probably known to all of you. Certain diseases seem to have a special tendency to re-

---

* Amongst which we may especially distinguish cerebral hæmorrhage, paralysis, and idiopathic gangrene.

appear in the offspring of those affected with them. And as this tendency may remain latent throughout the whole of life—that is, may never be called into activity by circumstances,— we get instances of "atavism;" in which the disease of an ancestor reappears in his or her grandchild, without visibly involving the immediate parent of the latter. In like manner, the tendency may only be exemplified by collateral branches (for example, uncles and aunts) in one generation, but equally affect the children of the healthier individuals (the nephews and nieces of the diseased ones) in the next generation. Hence we do not look exclusively to the parents of a given person, but rather to his family in general. And on the whole, the detection of any one of these "hereditary" complaints in his family history indicates that he has a higher liability to the same malady than the mass of the community, whose average mortality forms the basis of Life Assurance.

But it is obvious that the influence of an hereditary tendency to any such disease on the prospective duration of life, must depend (1), on the danger to life which the particular disease involves; and (2), on the degree on which its transmitted or congenital liability exceeds that risk which every individual runs of acquiring it. And the difficulty of exactly estimating these two points generally reduces our knowledge to little more than conjectures, which, however great their practical value, have but little scientific accuracy.

Of all the hereditary complaints, *pulmonary tubercle* or *consumption* is that which has the most important relation to Life Assurance. Careful inquiry entitles me to conjecture that the mortality from this disease, among Lives properly selected, does not exceed one-tenth of its average share in the general mortality of the whole population, as shown by the Registrar-General's returns.* And though much of this difference is ascribable to the class from which such lives are taken, and to the personal examination itself, yet much of it must also be attributed to the care which is usually exercised in inquiring into the history of this disease in the family of proposers for Assurance.

There is no tabular information as yet collected that affords satisfactory grounds for any exact estimate as to the frequency of hereditary consumption. Accurately to diagnose the disease is often so difficult, that it is by no means every

---

* I base this statement chiefly on my own experience as Physician to a large Assurance Society.

observer on whose statements we can rely. For example, nobody who is conversant with the details of sickness and death among the poor, can suppose that in the many thousand infants annually registered as dying of consumption, the statement is always (or even generally) based on a careful physical examination of the chest during life by an accomplished auscultator, much less by dissection after death. Mere inquiries of unprofessional persons respecting other members of their family affected with this disease are accompanied with a still greater (though somewhat kindred) vagueness. Some suppose consumption and decline to be quite distinct; and answer with a negative your question about the former, because they have heard the latter referred to. Others speak of asthma, bronchitis, pleurisy, and inflammation of the chest, in perfect ignorance that these terms may, and often do, conceal the primary tubercular disease on which they immediately depend.

The latency of the predisposition already referred to involves us in another and equally serious difficulty. If we only search amongst the fathers and mothers of our cases, we shall certainly overlook a great many well-marked instances of transmission. But the disease itself is so frequent a cause of death, as to produce about 1 death in 7, or 15 per cent. of the whole mortality. Hence, enlarging the sphere of our inquiries in any given family soon increases the chances of our meeting with this disease to a degree that makes it all but impossible for us not to detect it in some relative.

For example, let us suppose the person who is the subject of our inquiry can afford us information respecting his father and mother; and the two brothers and sisters, as well as the father and mother, of each of these parents. Here, within this circle of closest consanguinity, are ten persons:—namely, two parents, four uncles and aunts, and four grandparents,—of whom, on an average, one and a half will have died of consumption. Hence, except in numbers exceeding this average, mere deaths by consumption afford no very safe conclusion.

My own inquiries among Hospital patients decidedly consumptive, within this circle of relationship, are summed up by the statement, that 90 per cent. had lost some one of the above relatives by what appeared to be the same disorder; and that, instead of one and a half out of ten (the average mortality), about three and a half had thus died.

I think, therefore, we must deduce that, however strong the hereditary influence of this disease, we have no right to condemn a person on the mere suspicion which a single instance in his family can afford. And I venture (though, I acknowledge, with reluctance) to offer you the following practical rules, which may guide you in fixing the degree of this apparent influence that can justify such a proceeding.

There is an impression (which is favoured by some well-known facts in the physiology of generation) that the tendency to phthisis is more likely to be transmitted by a mother than by a father thus diseased. Other things being equal, it may be so. But any such preponderance is often outweighed by a strong and predominant likeness of the offspring to either of these parents. For such an external likeness may well be supposed associated with an equal similarity of constitution, especially where it involves the framework of the thoracic cavity in which the disease chiefly shows itself. Hence, though the father of our subject of inquiry may have died of decline, still if he himself takes strongly after his mother, this resemblance to the healthier branch of his ancestry goes far to nullify the injurious suspicions which his father's death might otherwise have excited.

Where, in addition to a consumptive father or mother, you find a consumptive brother or sister, you will do better to decline the Life. The influence of a consumptive grandfather or grandmother, in addition to a father or mother, is rather less decisive; because, as you will observe, it is more dilute.

Where the father and mother have both died of consumption we can have still less doubt. In the preceding cases the probabilities of a consumptive tendency have been merely accumulated. But in this they are multiplied;—so multiplied that (as is well known) such unhappy unions sometimes end a family, by the successive deaths of every one of the offspring with this dreadful disease.

Where neither father nor mother have died of consumption, and where the deaths, collaterally and upwards, within the above limits, are equally free from this disease, it will often be very hard to say what influence the deaths of brothers and sisters should have. You had better, I think, allow for numbers; and, for example, not permit one or even two deaths by consumption, out of ten brothers or sisters, to decide you against an individual otherwise healthy. And, beside allowing for likeness (or the reverse) between the deceased relative and the subject of examination, you must recollect the influence of intemperance in the male, and of the few dangerous years that immediately follow puberty in the unmarried female. It will also be well to inquire at what ages the consumptive brothers or sisters have died. Where they have all died, for instance, at or under the age of 25, and your subject of inquiry has already attained the age of 40, his danger has greatly diminished.

Indeed, in all cases, this diminution of the risk of consumption with advancing age must be systematically allowed for. The decrease is such, that at 40, half the danger is over; and at 50, three-fourths in the male, four-fifths in the female. At 60, but one-fourteenth remains, even in the male, in whom we may regard the liability throughout the whole of life as about one-fourth greater than in the female (5 to 4).

Any attempt to estimate the importance of another of the hereditary diseases—*insanity*—offers us difficulties even greater than those of consumption. But as the disease itself shortens life to a much smaller extent, the tendency to it seems less significant. The circumstances of the madness supposed to be transmitted would often guide us to a better estimate of its influence than any arbitrary rule could afford. One exception, however, it is important to notice. Persons are often said to have died mad, when, on inquiry, the insanity turns out to have been senile dementia;— a form of mental alienation that is sometimes little more than a variety of old age, and hence no valid argument against the longevity of a descendant.

With just as brief a notice we may pass over a number of other maladies, such as cancer, gout, and heart-disease, which are known to be sometimes hereditary. To exercise much influence on our present object, the disease must coincide in two or more relatives; and even then it will rarely be available for more than a limited aid to our decision.

Personal History.—Turning from the account given by the subject of our examination respecting his family, we must next inquire into his own history:—a category in which we may not only include his personal habits, but may conveniently (though incorrectly) group many of the circumstances in which he is placed at the time of being examined.

Of these habits, there is none into which it is more important to inquire than *temperance;* and none respecting which it is more difficult to obtain trustworthy information.

Merely to ask a person "Are you temperate?" is a waste of speech. For it may be laid down as a rule, that few men will allow themselves to be otherwise, whatever their transgressions in this respect. Indeed, there is no particular in which the mass of mankind feel less scruple in misleading our inquiries by what seem to be more or less direct untruths.

It may guard you against some of these subterfuges to remind you, that temperance means temperance in eating as well as drinking; that a man has been known to describe his habits as regular on the strength of being regularly intoxicated; that others state themselves to be temperate, because, though always partially stupefied by alcohol, they are rarely downright comatose; that others regard themselves as temperate, considering their circumstances, allowing for their temptations, comparing themselves with their neighbours; that

ers boldly pledge themselves to the same assertion after a week or two of careful preparation for your scrutiny. In short, that if you take such statements at their real value, they are best arranged in the formula, $x=0$.

In point of fact, the only way to get a reasonably correct answer of this kind is, never to ask for it directly, but to regard it as a summary of the information derived from your own questions and observations.

In respect to your questions, you must find out (as nearly as possible) both the quality and the quantity of fermented fluids the person habitually consumes. This, with a little tact, it is not difficult to do. And, of course, if you discover that he takes a gallon of beer, or a bottle or two of wine, daily, with a glass of spirits in the evening (increased to two or three in the company of friends)—why you will receive any asseveration of temperance with which he may have prefaced such a confession, *cum grano salis.*

As regards your observations (in speaking of which here I am sacrificing the regularity of my remarks for the sake of their practical usefulness), you must all of you be familiar with the appearance that habitual intemperance produces in its victims.

Mere gluttony does not carry such distinct or independent marks as the drunkenness with which it is generally associated. But the crapulous drunkard and the dram-drinker have much in common. The chief characteristics one can briefly express in words, are the fiery, unctuous skin, with its secretions reeking with volatile fatty acids; the red and ferretty eyes, with their fitful glare, rather than gleam; the furred tongue, the fœtid breath, and the trembling limbs, that often announce the impression made by the copious habitual ingestion of alcohol on the stomach and nervous system respectively.

Are Teetotallers good Lives? Merely in respect to the fact of their Teetotalism they decidedly are. They are spared (especially in the lower ranks) many of the temptations of their fellows, and thus many chances of disease; they are less likely (because, I believe, less able) to work themselves to death; and beside this, the mere fact of their having so much prudence and self-restraint is one that will probably enable them to surround themselves with many of those comforts which really prolong life.

But the permanence of the ill effects produced by those habits that often precede Teetotalism, will frequently oblige us to reverse the above answer. I have seen quite enough to justify me in asserting that the reformed drunkard is not a good Life; and that (whatever may be the case as regards his moral nature) his repentance, as regards his physical constitution, often comes too late. Many months, or even years, of the most complete abstinence, scarcely suffice to restore his probabilities of existence to a level with those of the temperate user of alcohol. Setting aside the not inconsiderable chances of his relapsing into old habits, his constitution often seems to have a peculiarly treacherous character; its apparently robust health consuming away with unusual rapidity under a moderately severe attack of any acute disease.

Those laws of our physical existence which render light, air, and exercise, necessary conditions of health, are so well known to you, that I need hardly mention them, save to add, that in the large numbers of persons with which Life Assurance is concerned, they are even more essential to longevity than in any given individual. Hence, a man who practices a sedentary calling in a dark, low, ill-ventilated room, is *(cæteris paribus)* a bad Life, especially where there is any reason to suspect a phthisical taint. For such habits are, of all others, the most calculated to develop phthisis.*

But we must not overrate the value of exercise so as to fancy that it may with impunity be carried to excess. Late researches have shown that, even in the more active out-door callings, the amount of sickness, and the rapidity of death, coincide with the degree of toil and exposure they imply;—in short, that the human machine is worn out by overwork, as surely as any artificial apparatus we can construct. Hence though, in the middle ranks, an unusual liking for extreme physical exertion is often the mere expression of a robust frame, that is peculiarly calculated to support it, or even to benefit by it,—among our brethren, the sons of toil, who have no such option, the case is very different. To them, indeed, we may apply, with an altered but melancholy significance, the words of the Apostle—" bodily exercise profiteth little;"—just as, on the other hand, we may anticipate, in every mechanical invention that lightens their labour, another accession to the increasing duration of their life.

* An excellent illustration of this fact has been established by Dr. Guy, in the greater liability of compositors to this disease than the pressmen who work under the same roof.

The influence of special trades or employments on longevity is not yet known with sufficient accuracy to justify us in regarding them as specific causes of mortality, apart from the circumstances already alluded to. I shall therefore content myself with alluding to some of the more unhealthy avocations, without attempting to define the increase of risk they imply.

The most important are probably those in which persons are obliged to respire large quantities of pulverulent (and especially inorganic) substances. The grinders of Sheffield and Redditch used to be cut off by the pulmonary disorganization brought about by their inhaling the dust of stone and iron, with such frightful rapidity and certainty, that it seems almost incredible any civilised Christian community could have permitted this loss of life to continue, without exhausting all the resources of science and legislation in attempting its removal. Stonemasons, millers, and others, are exposed to a similar (though, of course, less remarkable) risk.

Great exposure to cold, great fatigue, and remarkable alternations of temperature, have a perceptible effect on the mortality of a class. The couriers of Russia are said to die young, exhausted by their constant travel. And the journeymen bakers of our own metropolis illustrate by their great mortality the results of night labour and unrest, acting in connexion with alternate confinement in a hot and close bakehouse, and exposure in the cold and wet streets.

The specific poisons made use of in some handicrafts are on the whole less dangerous to mere life. The lead, for example, used by painters, the mercury by looking-glass makers, or even the phosphorus employed by lucifer-match makers, scarcely seem (though I must beg you to accept this word in its strictest sense) to have much effect on the deaths of the whole class. Besides, their results would be generally traceable in the examination of the individual.

How remarkably, however, a careful inquiry may modify and extend our previous conjectures, is well seen in some results recently published by the Registrar-General. He finds that the mortality of the ordinary labourer successively rises in the classes of shoemakers, miners, bakers, and butchers, to reach its maximum in the tavern-keeper or publican, in whom it is about two-thirds (2·7 to 1·7) greater than in the labourer. I need say nothing to increase the significance of these facts;

or to add to the care with which, in examining a member of the tavern-keeping class, you are bound to inquire into his immunity from that intemperance to which his calling so peculiarly tempts him, and to which this very great additional risk is no doubt chiefly due.

Residence is another of those important circumstances which it is more convenient to consider at once in its phases of past, present, and future; unchanged and changed.

Mere differences in the place of abode within the limits of this country do not generally enter into the calculations of the medical examiner to a Life Assurance Society. It is only amongst the noisome and overcrowded dwellings of our urban poor, that the influence of unhealthy residence is sufficiently marked and measurable, to be an element in the probabilities of existence. And this class, I need scarcely say, is hardly likely to offer candidates for examination.

It is chiefly with respect to changes of climate that such considerations come into action. The native of a different climate comes here to reside, and you are asked whether his Life is as good as that of one of our own countrymen. Or the

Englishman is about to go abroad, and you have to determine whether his risks remain no greater than before.

Here it is convenient to distinguish between the constitutional effects of mere climate, and the risk of diseases more or less endemic to the inhabitants of a given locality. The latter you can only judge of by whatever information you may possess (or be able to acquire) respecting the place itself. The prevalence of ague at Galatz, or furuncle at Aleppo, or ophthalmia in Lower Egypt, are facts which you can only acquire each by each, as matters of specific information. And other things being equal, you would, of course, judge by the frequency and fatality of the endemic disease, how far it damaged the probabilities of life.

But there are certain general influences of climate, concerning which we can group our knowledge into something more akin to a law. The native of a warmer climate who seeks this country, runs a risk of pulmonic—and especially of tubercular—disease, which may be roughly regarded as hardly inferior to that of an hereditary tendency of ordinary intensity. This risk we may probably consider as less in the case of an immigrant from southern Europe, than in one from a much hotter climate, such as Central Asia or Africa. It may also be supposed to be diminished where the person has already resided here some years without obvious ill effects; both from such a lapse of time introducing that influence of age already alluded to, and also from its justifying us in the supposition of an immunity enjoyed by the individual.

The emigration of an Englishman to a much colder climate, though perhaps attended with more risk than is generally supposed, has a less definite effect; none, indeed, that can fairly influence us apart from that of the disease endemic to the particular locality.

As respects migration to a hotter climate, our knowledge is yet very imperfect. The diseases which such a change seems most likely to produce are chiefly those of the organs of digestion and assimilation. Hence any previous or existing lesion of these organs increases the risk incurred by a given individual. Fatigue, or exposure to excessive heat, and the danger of endemic disease, often form additional elements of the change, which, however important, vary with every particular case.

Apart from these there remain but two circumstances of much account. One is, that the earlier after the completion of the epoch of puberty the person seeks these foreign climates, the better the acclimatisation that seems to occur, or the less the risk of his residence there. The other is the remarkable influence of temperance; which in hot climates is even more essential to health than in temperate or cold regions. The slighter and less perceptible effects of over indulgence in alcoholic liquors in a temperate climate—often mere dyspeptic ailments, the cause of which may remain unsuspected for years—are here exchanged for serious gastro-intestinal or hepatic diseases, that break up the system long before the usual epoch of those gouty attacks, by which the constitution of the Englishman at home resents such erroneous habits at the beginning of old age.

Practically, then, where your subject of examination is proceeding to India, you must look well to his age—relative as well as absolute: you must inquire what are his years, and see that nothing has made him virtually older than those years. Then satisfy yourself that his stomach and bowels (the latter especially) are habitually in good order, and that his liver and spleen are of healthy size. Inquire, to, whether he has ever had ague or jaundice. Lastly, you must not only find out whether he has ever been downright intemperate;

but also (if you can) whether he is strictly temperate. Of course, by temperance I do not mean total abstinence from alcoholic fluids; although, in India, the moderate use of beer and light wines ought almost to exclude all consumption of ardent spirits.

History of previous diseases.—It is scarcely necessary to state that there are few of the persons who come under our examination whose history is absolutely free from all disease of any kind. And this very fact makes it of great importance that we should determine, as far as possible, in what degree the different ailments from which the individual may have already suffered, diminish his expectancy of live.

1. There are some which indicate a tendency to dangerous disease, inasmuch as they are frequently either precursors of its occurrence, or even early symptoms of its existence.

Of these, pulmonary *hæmoptysis* is perhaps the most important. A large proportion of the persons who experience this symptom ultimately die of that pulmonary disease of which it is well known to be one of the earliest, as well as most dangerous, symptoms. The precise percentage in whom the symptom is devoid of this significance—in whom either the hæmorrhage is independent of the presence of tubercle, or the tubercular deposit fails to kill—remains quite unknown to us. And I do not see any advantage in burdening your memories with statements of the proportionate frequency of pulmonary hæmoptysis in ascertained phthisis; because, even assuming their accuracy, such figures reflect little light on the more important question as to how frequently pulmonary hæmoptysis ends in consumption. You must be content to know that it has this termination so frequently, that we are obliged pitilessly to exclude every person who has ever suffered from this symptom, from the benefits of ordinary Life Assurance.

I place before you this outline of your duty in all its naked harshness, because I believe such a way of stating it is, of all others, the most likely to make you conscientiously careful and accurate in filling up its details. You must carefully inquire into all the alleged cases of hæmoptysis that come before you; and assure yourselves, as far as possible, that they really were what they are supposed to have been. To specify the signs by which you would diagnose this fact would lead me too far from my subject, and would probably only repeat what has been already told you by my colleagues, the Lecturers on Clinical and on Systematic Medicine. Of course, when you find (as I have done before now, in making such inquiries) that the blood came from the gums or the stomach, or that it was a mere streak that might well have been derived from the trachea or larynx abraded in the act of coughing, you will not allow it to guide you to such a decision. But, on the whole, the *onus probandi* lies with the case itself; and if its circumstances fail to explain away the supposed hæmoptysis to your satisfaction, I venture to suggest your declining to recommend the Life.

Among circumstances that do not explain it away, let me mention the absence of phthisical taint in the family history; or the fact that the spitting of blood has been ascribed to some exertion shortly before its attack. Unless the time of the hæmoptysis absolutely coincided with that of some intense and prolonged exertion, such an explanation has little in its favour. And even supposing this to have been the case, I can scarcely regard it safe to accept such a Life, except where the appearance, the personal and family history, and the health of the patient for a long subsequent period, all coincide to enforce the view of its accidental origin.

In the same class of symptoms we may place evidence of those degenerative changes which so often accompany old age, and, indeed, constitute that relative senility which it is so important for us to appreciate and detect. You will, perhaps, think me stating a truism, to say that a person who has had aneurism, paralysis, or senile gangrene, is not a good life. But I have known instances in which medical examiners appear to have come to the opposite conclusion.

2. There are diseases which offer us a serious warning when they occur in a person's history, because they frequently involve damage to structures that are peculiarly essential to life. Thus the mention of acute rheumatism should always lead us to examine very carefully into the condition of the heart; and, if possible, to obtain a special report from the medical attendant of the person we are examining, with reference to the chief features of the attack. In like manner, the occurrence of dropsy, even many years before, should always render us suspicious of existing cardiac or renal mischief, and direct our inquiry especially to these organs.

3. There are maladies which increase the risk of other diseases more or less independent of themselves. Such a character especially belongs to many complaints of the respiratory organs, which leave behind them a variable amount of permanent damage in these important structures. Thus pleurisy, or pneumonia, even when they end in recovery, rarely disappear without inflicting some permanent injury on that portion of the lung which they have especially engaged. And if this portion be sufficiently large to constitute an important fraction of the whole respiratory structure, it is evident that any casual disease that may hereafter attack this organ is likely to be far more dangerous than where it involves lungs previously healthy. Indeed, in such a case, the mischief previously existing may (and often does) turn the wavering balance of life and death, and decide the latter event. But since it is not so much the history of disease, as the structural traces left behind it, upon which our calculations would be based, I may defer any fuller allusion to this point until it again claims our notice in speaking of the personal examination.

It may be useful, however, to caution you against receiving too implicitly the statements made by the subject of inquiry respecting the diseases he has gone through. In some cases the names given to the diseases are, perhaps, correct, and it is only our interpretation of their degree which makes them erroneous. But, in many instances, there can be no doubt that the nomenclature adopted is one such as the legitimate practitioner of medicine ought to relinquish to the quack. Thus a careful inquiry will sometimes entitle you to believe that the high-sounding titles of "inflammation of the kidneys," "inflammation of the liver," "inflammation of the bowels," have been attached to transient pains over the regions supposed to be occupied by these viscera;—pains perhaps due to lumbago or constipation respectively. In like manner the term "pleurisy" often refers to that slight degree of this malady which a mere stitch in the side occasionally entitles us to suspect. And "inflammation of the brain" is no very rare misnomer for the delirium of continued fever.

4. There are maladies which are suspicious features of a person's history from their liability to return; from their predisposing the constitution to their recurrence. Such are gout, asthma, dropsy, dysentery, gastric ulcer, and many others too nu-

merous to mention. Of course, in speaking of this liability to recur, I am supposing that they are completely absent at the time of examination; a fact which you would have to establish by the rules presently to be hinted at. But you must recollect that their worst features are sometimes latent; and hence that periods which seem to be real intermissions, followed by their return, have no real title to this name. Thus gout or dropsy may be associated with diseased kidney; such as can be readily detected by a careful examination of the urine in the intervals of the attacks, and is attended with a specific effusion into the joints or areolar tissue respectively. Asthma may leave its mark in the shape of emphysema between the paroxysms. And dysentery or gastric ulcer may be indicated, under similar circumstances, by such symptoms as diarrhœa, or vomiting, on the slightest error of diet.

5. And, lastly, there are certain diseases which we may not only contrast with the preceding in this respect, but may regard as almost accidental. These are the exanthemata, in which (for our present purposes) we may include the typhoid and typhus fevers. My own impression is, that it scarcely argues more against a person's constitu-

tion to have had any one of these disorders, than to have received a fracture of his arm or leg. Different individuals have bones of different strength and thickness, and therefore of different fragility; but all may be broken by violence. And, in like manner, any person who is sufficiently exposed to infection is pretty sure to catch any one of these maladies.

Indeed, as most of them generally occur at some time of life, and are (on the whole) more dangerous as life advances, it is rather an advantage (in other words, an increase of the probabilities of life) for any individual to have already undergone them. For such a fact not only indicates a good constitution, but, from the rarity of their occurring twice in the same person, also lessens the risk of these diseases hereafter. Idiopathic erysipelas, however, we must exclude from this statement; though where it recurs often, its later attacks are rarely very dangerous. I need only add, in concluding this part of the subject, that you must remember the renal affection which often complicates scarlet fever, and the chronic disease of the kidney it sometimes leaves behind it; and that it is part of your duty to acquire specific evidence either of small-pox, or of successful (or at least repeated) vaccination.

Personal Examination.—The personal examination which forms the third and last part of our inquiry is the most difficult, as well as the most strictly professional, part of our duty. Hitherto we have had to do little more than interpret facts which almost any one might have collected. Now the very facts themselves are such as it requires the trained observation of a physician to detect and appreciate. And hence the few remarks I have to offer must be looked upon, less as rules for your guidance, than as hints which may assist to sharpen the keenness of your scrutiny in a few of the most important respects.

And, firstly, as to *age*. The person under examination is always required to adduce evidence of his age; indeed, the truth of such evidence forms the very basis of the contract between himself and the Assurance Society. With this his real age, it will always be your duty to contrast his apparent age, and carefully to note any discrepancy between the two. Experience alone can acquaint you with the various details on which an opinion of this kind must be founded—the thousand trifles of form and feature, of gait and manner, that sometimes make up the circumstantial evidence of commencing decay. And you must look to a combination of these

D

details, rather than to an unusual prominence of any one or two of them, for correct information on this head.*

Akin to the appearances by which we generally infer the age of the person under examination, are some characters which are always worthy of notice; namely, the complexion, the build, and the weight.

Weight is of course always to be considered relatively to height.

As a rule, it may be laid down that an adult male in good health, 66 inches in stature, ought to weigh rather more than ten stones, or 140 pounds avoirdupois. And for every inch above and below this height we may respectively add and subtract about five pounds.

The variations specific to the individual (often indeed to a family) take so wide a range, that it is difficult to assign them any precise limit. But as a rule, 20 per cent., or one-fifth, is almost the maximum variation compatible with health. In other words, if our subject of 66 inches in stature weighed more than twelve stones, or less than eight, we should be entitled to look upon him with great suspicion.

* Taken alone, for example, even the *arcus senilis* is scarcely a sufficient evidence of relative old age.

But it is not so much a permanent or habitual variation from this standard that we have to suspect, as a rapid or sudden alteration of it. If our subject of 66 inches in height appeared, on close inquiry, to have gained or lost in a few months as little as fifteen or twenty pounds, this would be a far stronger feature against his Life than a constant divergence of double or treble that amount from our imaginary standard.

The suspicions derivable from such rapid approaches towards emaciation or corpulence may be usefully checked by an inquiry into one or two circumstances. Towards the close of early adult life, you are aware that corpulence generally increases; indeed, partly from the cessation of growth, partly from the more sedentary habits into which many persons lapse about this period, the epoch from 30 to 40 generally renders a healthy person of either sex considerably stouter and heavier:— what our allies call "*un bel homme*" in the man, and what the first gentleman in Europe elegantly described as "fat, fair, and forty" in the other sex. Conversely, you will of course recollect how rapidly a course of temperance and severe exercise, such as almost renews the youth of those who engage in it, can reduce the weight of the body to at least our imaginary limit of 20 per cent. Thus, in the delightfully esoteric language of the Sporting Journals, that eminent pugilist, the Tutbury Pet, is announced to "fight ten stone," when, perhaps, but a few days before the event on which the eyes of all England are supposed to be fixed, the weight of his debauched frame is little less than twelve stones.

Excluding such influences, as we may easily do, emaciation points at some serious check to assimilation, or increase of waste, such as consumption or diabetes. In like manner, the rapid access of corpulence is generally due to intemperance, or to the privation of proper exercise; and in this point of view, may be equally regarded as a sign of disease, or as a mark of premature old age.

Colour is an appearance which is often of the greatest importance. A florid and uniform facial colour is usually associated with that habitual activity of the skin which is the result of a life of active exercise in the open air. In persons of delicate skin, solar heat has a somewhat similar effect; though here the red colour is not only less intense, but is generally of a much browner tint. How much a ruddy colour may be heightened (or even to some extent simulated) by the effect of alcoholic potations, no Englishman who reads Shakspeare can be ignorant of. And the usual site of the greatest redness of this kind I need hardly specify in a populous city like this, where we may meet a Bardolph in almost every crowded street.

There is one modification of facial colour, however, which deserves a momentary allusion; since I think it may sometimes guide you to a valuable conjecture, such as may be at once confirmed or refuted by further inquiry. We sometimes see the cheeks of a middle-aged person coloured—not by a flush of mere redness, such as can be produced by the glimmering of blood in the minutest capillaries of the skin—but by streaks of distended bloodvessels themselves, which give the middle of the cheek a peculiar mottled appearance.

Whenever this streaky congestion is contrasted with great pallor of the skin generally, and especially of the surrounding integuments, you will do well to examine carefully into the state of the urine. This physiognomy (which my brief description may perhaps indicate, but certainly not depict) has often attracted my attention in a crowded out-patient room: and (taken in conjunction with the soft velvety skin by which

Nature strives to eliminate urea from the system in such cases of obstructed renal secretion) has enabled me to predict the presence of albumen in the urine.

The opposite complexion, or pallor, is just as grave a feature in any given case. Supposing that it is too intense or too recent to be regarded as an individual or family peculiarity, and that it is not explained by the habits of the subject of your examination—for I may remind you that dark rooms and close hot air will blanch a ruddy face, just as they would the coloured parts of a plant— it becomes a very suspicious sign. I shall not enumerate the diseases by which such pallor is most likely to be produced: they are too many and too diverse to be usefully cited here. Loss of blood, deficient formation of this fluid, or excessive waste of the tissues it furnishes, may all give rise to this hue; though with certain modifications in each of these cases respectively. But from the frequency of pulmonary consumption in this climate, the cachexia which such paleness denotes is perhaps more frequently due to this disease than to any other malady.

Deformities require careful notice, even when the immediate effects of the disease or injury that may have caused them have long passed away, and the general health is completely restored.

Thus, as regards the *chest*, its shape is rarely much altered, by disease or injury, without a considerable diminution both of its capacity and mobility. Each of these losses entails a corresponding damage upon the function of the chest as the organ of respiration. And though this damage may not reduce the action of the organ below what can effect all the breathing ordinarily necessary, it becomes much more serious when any disease (however temporary) engages another portion of lung. For then the unaffected structures, which might otherwise have compensated, by their increased energy, for that impairment of the organ as a whole which such disease implies, are perhaps unable to do so, owing to the additional impairment produced by the deformity. Hence the thoracic deformity left by pleurisy or emphysema, or even by distortion of the spine, may render fatal a limited attack of bronchitis or pneumonia, such as a healthy person would have easily recovered from. And when we consider what a large fraction such diseases of the respiratory organs form of the whole causes of death in this climate—or, in other words, considering their moderate fatality, how very unlikely any person is altogether to escape them during a long series of years—we shall find reason to conclude that the presence of such deformity implies what must, in the mass of cases, amount to a serious diminution of the probabilities of life.

How far the deformity present in any given instance is likely to injure the function of the chest as an organ of respiration, can of course only be determined by its nature and amount, as well as by other circumstances that are sure to vary in each particular case. With proper limitations, great aid in such an inquiry is afforded by the Spirometer, an instrument to which we shall allude again by-and-bye.

There is one deformity of the chest, however, which we may notice, as being rarely a valid objection against those in whom it is found uncomplicated. This is the peculiar shape to which the term "pigeon-breasted" is generally applied; owing to the sternum being unusually projecting and the chest itself flattened on each side. This shape, which appears to be due to a want of proper hardness in the costal cartilages, and in the adjacent ends of the ribs prior to their ossification, and which I have found in several instances to be hereditary, can be shown by all ordinary tests (including the Spirometer) to inflict comparatively little damage on the capacity of the chest.

Deformity of the *pelvis* is of course not to be detected in an ordinary Life Office examination; save where it may be fairly inferred from the existence of considerable malformation in the adjacent segments of the spine. And though we can hardly go the length of the zealous French accoucheur, who thought that every village *curé* ought to possess an accurately graduated pelvimeter, and by its aid reject all female candidates for matrimony whose parturition would much endanger themselves or their offspring, yet there can be no doubt that, except in women past the age of child-bearing, the existence of much pelvic deformity affords sufficient grounds for rejecting a female Life.

Respecting the degree in which *hernia* impairs a person's expectancy of Life, it is difficult to say anything satisfactory. But that it does do so, the frequency with which strangulated hernia occurs as a cause of death in the registered mortality of the population, places beyond all doubt. The only questions are—Whether this increase of risk is such as to demand any extra premium? And if so, by what addition it may be compensated? Any answer to these questions, on accurate medical data, I confess myself utterly unable to afford you. And from the fact, that different Offices demand a high extra rate, a low extra rate, or none at all, I may presume that the majority of Actuaries have no definite numerical foundations for the graduated hernia premiums their respective Offices allot to the subjects of such deformities.

A few remarks, however, may be added to this confession of ignorance. Firstly, always examine the alleged hernia. I have sometimes found that the supposed rupture was an undescended testicle; sometimes had reason to conclude that the previous hernia had been removed by a well-adjusted truss worn during many years; and twice, could specifically assert that the patient had never had rupture at all.* Secondly, hernia is more dangerous in the female than in the male: partly from its being usually femoral instead of inguinal; much more, I believe, from the concealment which modesty

---

* One of these supposed cases of hernia had been lately discovered by a notorious practitioner of homœopathy, who, no way disconcerted by his patient's acquainting him with the result of my examination, gravely asserted, that the tumour had been suddenly removed by the globules he had prescribed.

leads women to adopt respecting its occurrence or aggravation. Thirdly, the avocation of the subject of hernia is worth considering; since, if it implies violent bodily exertion, it increases the risk of strangulation. Fourthly, the duration of the hernia does not seem to have any effect upon its danger, sufficiently marked or frequent to guide our conjectures; a recent hernia often becomes strangulated, and even a large old hernia not unfrequently undergoes the same accident. Fifthly, the constant wearing of a well-adapted truss is of course a favourable feature in any given case; especially where this treatment, in a young subject, has already reduced the size of the tumour.

The effect of the loss of a limb, or a special sense, it is rarely necessary to estimate. Amputation of a limb for disease is said to confer an increased risk of visceral—especially of pulmonary—disease. But here the previous malady would itself enter into our calculations, as well as the present health (including any appearances of latent mischief) of the person examined. Amputation for injury or accident is also said to be often followed by a plethoric state, and a tendency to corpulence, that are attended with increased risk to the constitution. These, however, would also be visible facts, that could scarcely escape notice.

And in respect to these mutilations, as well as to complete blindness, deafness, and the like, we may sum up their other chief indirect effects, in the general statement:—that whatever interferes with the exercise natural to a healthy individual, or deprives him of the proper guards against accident which nature furnishes, of course increases his risk of disease and injury respectively. But how far it will do so must be judged of from the details of each case—in other words, the habits and circumstances of the individual. In the affluent classes, the care and attention that wealth can secure, often reduce the influence of such accidents to a minimum that may practically be overlooked altogether.

The influence of *open ulcers* or *sores* is much more serious, and will generally oblige us to decline any Life in which they are present. The elements of the increase they add to the average risk are not very difficult to imagine. They imply a drain on the constitution which, as age advances, and Nutrition declines, may become a dangerous or fatal one. Their closure sometimes brings about visceral disease, by revulsion of morbid action to internal organs. They indicate, in the main, either a bad original constitution, or hurtful habits of life —often both. Lastly, while they may at any time take on an increased action, so as to threaten the limb or the life, they involve no inconsiderable risk of infection with erysipelas; if indeed they do not sometimes form a channel for the reception of other exanthematous disorders.

The detection of latent or nascent disease is the last (but not least) object of our examination.

It is obvious that, even supposing the art of diagnosis were perfect, the most skilful physician would be unable to satisfy himself of the complete absence of disease, save by a sedulous examination of the whole body. But I need scarcely tell you that so stringent a procedure is neither necessary nor practicable in an ordinary examination for Life Assurance purposes. In short, the inquiry we have to conduct is directed towards such diseases as are especially calculated to shorten life; and the examination of the subject of Assurance is generally restricted to what may be undergone without much difficulty, and without any injury to ordinary feelings of delicacy.

Distinguishing the four chief groups of organs— the nervous, the digestive, the respiratory, and the circulatory—it is evident that the means already suggested have, in the case of some of them, left us little more to inquire about.

Assuming, for instance, that our subject of examination has no nervous disease entering into his history, if we find that his habits are active, his pursuits such as require sanity of mind and body, his face devoid of all traces of paralysis, his gait and gestures vigorous and healthy; these circumstances almost suffice of themselves to exclude all suspicion of cerebral or spinal disease, such as the most sedulous examination of the skull or spine could detect.

In like manner let us suppose that, with an equally healthy history, our subject of inquiry has always been temperate, that his digestion is good, and that his bowels are habitually regular. We look at his tongue, and find that its healthy appearance silently confirms the statements it has verbally made. We examine the belly, through the ordinary dress, and find that the liver and spleen are not enlarged, that the abdomen itself is not unduly corpulent for the age of the individual: and we have almost as effectually excluded the presence of serious disease of the digestive organs.

In like manner, with respect to the urinary

apparatus, careful inquiry will often give us so healthy a history of its function as to allow us to dispense with all further examination, not only of the organs themselves, but even of their secretion. It is only where gout, scarlatina, dropsy, or some other disease or appearance of a like suspicious character, specially directs our research toward these structures, that we need alarm or annoy our subject of examination by insisting on any further inquiry.

It is to the viscera of the chest that our observation may be most usefully directed; both from the frequency with which constitutional disease implicates these organs, and from the comparative facility with which such disease may be detected.

In the male, the ordinary dress generally affords few obstacles to a sufficiently searching examination. The person stands nearly upright, leaning with his back against the wall; and throws backward his coat and waistcoat so as to expose the under clothing that covers the chest and upper part of the belly.

We now examine into (1,) the shape of the chest; (2,) the nature and extent of its movements; (3,) the relative situation of the lungs and heart, as determined by percussion of its walls; (4,) the character of the sounds given out by the pulmonary regions of the chest under the same test; (5,) the vocal thrill felt on applying the hand to the same regions while the subject of inquiry is speaking; (6,) the character of the sounds of breathing, as ascertained by auscultation; and (7,) the character (including the force, timbre, and rhythm) of the cardiac sounds under the same test; with these we compare (8,) the frequency of the pulse; and, (9,) of the breathing.

It is of course impossible to mention here all the varieties of information thus revealed. I shall only allude to one or two of the most important.

Few would overlook the remarkable deformity sometimes produced by pleurisy, where one side of the chest gradually contracts around the condensed and atrophied lung, remaining shrunken, motionless, dull to percussion, and almost useless for the purposes of respiration. But those smaller degrees of the same state, in which the injured portion is but a fraction of the whole lung, are often associated with so little deformity, that anything short of careful examination might allow them to escape notice. Even here, however, we may generally find the diseased part indicated by a flattening of the convex ribs, a dullness to percussion, and a diminished respiratory murmur, after the more striking indications of disease have long disappeared.

The evidence of chronic deposit in the lungs (synonymous, in the majority of cases, with *tubercle*) is of course less characteristic; varying with the rapidity of its deposit, its amount, and its diffusion throughout the chest. But as it is not so much the diagnosis of phthisis, as the signs of its earliest access, with which we are here concerned, we may assume that the deposit is scanty and scattered. In such cases the chest is narrow, especially above; and the shoulder-blades are lower, and nearer to each other, than they should be; its movements are diminished; its sound to percussion is duller than natural. And as regards the vocal thrill, and the vocal and breathing sounds heard by auscultation, the kind of information we get may be summed up in the statement that (except in those rare instances in which the deposit is uniformly dispersed, in exceedingly small masses) these signs are irregular and variable—in one word, *heterogeneous*—in different parts of the lungs; instead of being regular, even and homogenous, as they are in health, in spite of the most striking individual peculiarities. The broken sound of inspiration, the long one of expiration, and the various signs of solidification or cavity, we need hardly mention.

The signs of *emphysema* are even more important, because a moderate degree of this structural lesion may not only be unsuspected by the subject of inquiry, but is quite compatible with an absence of all other symptoms at the time of examination. Indeed, such persons are often regarded by the ignorant as having remarkably fine chests. Here the chest is unnaturally deep from before backwards, as well as from above downwards; and, in extreme cases, contracted in either hypochondrium. The shoulders are raised. The movements of the sternum are much diminished; breathing being affected chiefly by the diaphragm. The unnaturally resonant or tympanitic sound given out by percussion under the clavicles, is contrasted with a deficiency of inspiratory murmur in the same region. The enlarged lung overlaps the heart, usurps the space in which the point of this latter organ ought to render the surface dull to percussion by its contact, and often transfers its visible pulsation to the upper part of the epigastrium. And the liver is often similarly displaced downwards.

The influence of a *hump-back* varies with the nature and site of the spinal distortion. But though it often reverses the effect of emphysema in the particulars last mentioned, it generally resembles this lesion in the diaphragmatic character of the breathing;—rarely in any diminution of respiratory murmur over the more motionless ribs.

The detection of *cardiac disease* by auscultation demands (like the diagnosis of the preceding pulmonary lesions) the possession of a high degree of practical diagnostic skill in the examiner—skill such as no cursory remarks of mine would aid you in attaining. As a rule, we first inquire, by percussion, whether the heart is enlarged, so as to claim an undue contact with the thoracic parietes, and push aside the lung or lungs. We then feel its impulse, and ascertain whether this also is of natural intensity and local extent. Lastly, we listen to its sounds: the dull systolic beat, coinciding with the impulse; and the sharp click, produced mainly by the sudden tension of the semilunar valves.

The varieties of these sounds compatible with a perfectly healthy state of the circulation, do not require much notice. The first, or systolic sound, varies, however, much more than the second; the character of which may be regarded as tolerably constant. The physiological (and even pathological) reasons for the contrast I must not here enter into.

Their rhythm, or relative duration and succession, is nearly as important as their character; although less easy to verify when but slightly modified.

Practically, however, you must not imagine that there are many instances in which auscultation, however carefully conducted, entitles you to reject a Life otherwise a good one, by detecting cardiac disease. In the majority of cases the information thus acquired is either quite satisfactory, or if suspicious, requires to be checked by that additional evidence which is derivable from family and personal history, and symptoms. And were we to consider it quite apart from these symptoms, it would occasionally lead us into much perplexity, if not error.

In other words, the early diagnosis of even such structural maladies as phthisis, or valvular disease of the heart, is much more frequently effected by constitutional symptoms than by physical signs. And, as regards mere auscultation, it is sometimes very difficult to determine whether the sounds heard are those of cardiac disease, or of a heart structurally healthy, but functionally excited by the nervous agitation of an examination.

Thus, as respects phthisis, it often happens that long before any definite evidence of structural disorder can be obtained by the most sedulous examination of the chest itself, the symptoms sufficiently reveal the coming (or rather the existing) mischief. The sufferer, even when retaining all his ordinary habits, becomes paler, loses weight, is perceptibly thinner: his pulse and respiration rise from about 65 and 16 per minute, to 90 or 100, and 25 or 30, respectively. He feels so much dyspnœa on exertion, that he can no longer walk or run rapidly, and is rendered quite breathless by quickly mounting a flight of stairs. While—to say nothing of the characteristic physiognomy, the brilliant eye, the pearly conjunctiva, the haggard but excited face—the spasmodic working of the nostrils in respiration reveals a state of dyspnœa, probably pulmonary, which tells the same tale as the above symptoms and history.

It is in such cases that the *Spirometer* is most useful as an aid to diagnosis. Even at this early stage of the disease, the tubercular deposit, however scanty in quantity, and diffuse in situation, rarely fails to damage the efficiency of the lungs as an organ of respiration. And hence it reduces the " vital capacity"—that is, the maximum expiration of the lungs in cubic inches of air—to about 25 or 30 per cent. below the standard of health.*

The use of this instrument offers no difficulties such as may not be easily either obviated or allowed for. It is applicable chiefly to the male, during the period of vigorous life that intervenes between the age of 15 and 50. Of course, it testifies equally to the damage inflicted by all structural disease that obliterates the cavity, or prevents the movement, of the respiratory organ: and hence it affords no inference as to the true

* The following details are subjoined for the convenience of those readers who may not be able to refer to any physiological treatise containing the descriptions and statements which the audience to whom this Lecture was delivered had been made acquainted with by the Lectures on Respiration in the Physiological Course.

My own observations among the class ordinarily presenting themselves for assurance, induce me to estimate that the healthy male, from 15 to 50 years of age, and of average weight (10 stone) and height (66 inches), has a vital capacity of about 200 cubic inches. For every inch above and below this stature, between 72 and 60 inches, we may respectively add and subtract about eight and a half cubic inches of capacity.

The variations of this vital capacity in respect of excess we need not notice. In regard of deficiency, about 15 per cent. below this standard may be considered as the minimum compatible with health. And even with less than this deficiency, it is advisable to seek for some explanation in the other circumstances of the case: such as advancing age, sedentary habits, or excess of weight; to which, either singly or in combination, such a decrease may be attributed.

pathology of that state of virtual apnœa it may indicate. By carefully watching the person under experiment, you can easily see whether he is making use of the apparatus aright; or whether the deficiency he seems to offer is only due to carelessness or clumsiness on his part.

The *pulse* is one of those evidences of disease which we shall do well to notice specially in reference to Life Assurance.

An inquiry into the force and frequency of the pulse forms an indispensable adjunct to auscultation in the diagnosis of cardiac disease. By

Of these three circumstances, the third is probably the most valid cause of the decrease; the second the least so. This influence of excess of weight upon vital capacity has been formulated by Dr. Hutchinson (On the Spirometer, p. 9) in the statement, that where it amounts to an excess of seven per cent. it begins to reduce capacity; and that every additional pound in excess, up to 35, takes off a cubic inch. I believe that, practically, this formula would rarely mislead us; although, physiologically, it is most important to distinguish between the limited influence of mere weight, and the marked local effect of abdominal corpulence on the movements of the chest. The effect of age, even apart from that of the corpulence and the sedentary habits with which it is often associated, is very considerable. My own researches induce me to regard Dr. Hutchinson's estimate—a decrease of about 10 per cent. only from the adult average in advancing to the age of 70—as far too small for that which generally obtains even in healthy persons. Indeed, at this period of life, I should not consider any deficiency short of 30 or 40 per cent. a sufficient ground of rejection in individuals otherwise unexceptionable.

mere examination into these points we may sometimes not only determine that the heart is structurally diseased, but may even predict the exact seat of the cardiac lesion. The full jerking pulse of aortic regurgitation, and the small and thready one of mitral disease, are probably familiar to most of you. And as the pulse is to some extent an index of the effect of the cardiac lesion on the circulation generally, it is a far better guide to the constitutional mischief produced, than the mere nature and amount of abnormal sound. A noisy bellows-sound by no means necessarily implies a worse disease of the heart than may be associated with a blowing that is nearly inaudible. But any serious affection of the pulse—such as a feeble, rapid, and fluttering impulse in the artery, corresponding to a similarly altered beat of the heart —points with much greater certainty to a dangerous character of the disease.

This apparent digression leads me to the most frequent source of embarrassment in these examinations: namely, the difficulty of distinguishing between nervousness and disease.

The majority of the individuals who come before the Medical Examiner to a Life Office, become more or less excited under the inquiry. And in some, the amount of the excitement is very great. The pulse rises in frequency; the heart beats violently against the wall of the chest; its sounds undergo considerable modifications; the breathing is sometimes accelerated; and, lastly, the general agitation of manner and gesture that accompanies these symptoms, occasionally amounts to downright tremor, and involuntary muscular movements.

The best method of detecting mere nervous excitement is a very simple one: namely, to prolong (or, if need be, repeat) the interview until the agitation it produces has somewhat subsided. Thus, however excited a person may be on entering a room, and however violently and rapidly his pulse may be beating, you have but to keep your finger on his wrist, while you soothe his anxiety, or distract his attention to some other topic, and you will generally find that the pulse becomes slower, fuller, and more natural for several beats together, even if its agitation do not permanently subside. Or, in a very nervous subject, you may repeat the examination of the pulse at a further stage of the interview with similar satisfactory results.

The same rule will apply to the effect of mental

agitation on the impulse and sounds of the heart. The violent throbbing impulse, the rushing (if not blowing) first sound, and the concealment or partial suppression of the second sound, which such excitement can produce, generally diminish remarkably in the course of a few minutes, even where they do not altogether disappear. And I need hardly say that in these cases all evidence of dilatation is absent. In some instances, however, it is only by repeated examination, and by a careful collation of the history and habits, as well as the symptoms, of the subject of inquiry, that we can satisfy ourselves of the merely nervous character of the other abnormal signs.

Excessive frequency or slowness of the pulse (which we may define as more than 85 or less than 50 per minute) is not common. Where present, we have to inquire whether it is known to have been habitual; and if so, for how long. It is only where it constitutes the sole symptom of a suspicious nature, and is utterly unconnected with any history of disease presumably cardiac, or any presumable tendency to phthisis, that we can safely regard it as the mere peculiarity of a healthy individual. The healthy deviation is, I think, more frequently towards a diminished than an increased rapidity: taking 70 as the mean frequency of the pulse per minute in the male adult, it certainly is so.*

It may not be uninteresting if I point out some other peculiarities in the pulse, as occasionally susceptible of easy explanation. The rate of nutrition and the supply of blood being both regulated by the exertion of a particular limb or organ, you will expect to find the pulse of the hale and robust working man what physicians of the school of Sangrado used to call "a strong jerking pulse, that would bear depletion." And conversely, the small and delicate hand that is never used for hard work has a proportionably "small" pulse. In like manner, a subcutaneous course of the radial artery or its volar branch, produce a pulse that has before now been mistaken for a "hard" one, and reduced by bleeding. Finally, within the last few months, I have seen one or two instances in which the radial artery (and therefore the pulse) was without any single efficient representative in the fore-arm of one side.

The intermittent pulse is the last and most

* An abnormal slowness of pulse points our suspicion chiefly towards cerebral disease—probably, we might say, in the medulla oblongata in the vicinity of the roots of the pneumogastric nerve.

important variety to which we may allude. It is sometimes habitual from birth; once or twice I have known it thus congenital in two or more healthy members of the same family. It is sometimes produced by green tea or tobacco; sometimes (I think, more rarely) by dyspepsia, independent of these deleterious agents. Lastly, it is sometimes an important element of relative old age — coinciding with a general degeneration of the arteries, or even preceding death by angina pectoris, or other allied diseases of the heart.

I am disposed to conjecture that, as a rule, the healthier or merely symptomatic varieties of intermittent pulse possess characters that would often serve as a more or less specific distinction. At least, of cases probably referable to this category, the majority have shown me what were quite consentaneous beats of the whole heart, the only flaw of the cardiac action consisting in the prolongation of some single diastole; prior to which, the last (or, at any rate, the penultimate) systole seemed much stronger than usual. While I have found the decayed or aged heart give irregular (and *quasi* divided) sounds, when carefully auscultated, though the pulsations seemed single at the wrist: and exhibit intermissions that were not preceded by any unusually powerful impulse—oftener by deficient impulse—at the chest or along the radial artery. But I believe the exceptions to this rule are too numerous to allow much stress to be laid upon it.

On the whole, it may be laid down that this symptom always requires something like an explanation, even in young and healthy subjects. And I have been able to collect some interesting cases which seem to prove that where of comparatively recent occurrence, in persons either absolutely or relatively old, it is ample ground for an unconditional rejection, in the absence of every other morbid sign or symptom of cardiac disease. And where (as is often the case in old persons) it is accompanied by a tortuous and inelastic state of the arteries generally, or by a gouty history, or by appearances of habits that have been free (though not in the ordinary sense intemperate), this rule will still be more applicable.

Insanity is a state which, whether actually present, or likely to obtain, as shown by family or personal history, constitutes a grave objection to the acceptance of a Life.

It has, indeed, been doubted how far insanity ought to be regarded as a disease shortening life.

And I presume the numbers of lunatics who attain old age have been supposed to countenance this doubt.

But all researches into the mortality of lunatics conclusively show that their probabilities of life are much less than those of sane persons at corresponding ages. And when we consider the large proportion of cases in which these mental maladies are associated with visible lesions of one of the organs most essential to life; the frequency with which such unhappy persons commit suicide; and the numberless chances of accident, privations, or exposure, to which the state of their intellect renders them liable; we shall not be surprised to find that their deaths far (six times) exceed the average mortality of the community at large.

I cannot suggest any useful classification or distinction of the various forms of mental alienation with respect to Life Assurance. The more obviously structural diseases of the brain would perhaps correspond to the maximum of risk. But, practically, the causes of death just hinted at often render fatal cases in which, as a matter of mere medical prognosis, such a result might perhaps have least been expected. Careful medical and general treatment would probably afford the best chance of longevity; but these are contingencies we have little right to calculate.

It is, however, important to beware of attaching too much importance to all cases of insanity that may be detected in the family history of persons who are themselves free from any suspicion of the malady. A close inquiry has often shown me that the reported insanity of some older relative was really little more than that mitigated form of senile dementia which so frequently precedes death by old age. And I need hardly say that this variety of mental decrepitude is no valid objection to the Lives of other members of a family; indeed, supposing it only to occur at an advanced age, is rather in favour of their longevity.

The state of the uterine functions will not require much allusion. The non-appearance of the catamenia at the proper age, or their abnormal interruption for a longer or shorter period during any part of menstrual life, would constitute a very important symptom, but one which would require to be carefully collated with the other circumstances of the case before any definite value could be assigned to it. Impending pregnancy does not much influence Assurances effected for the whole term of life, save where there are special reasons (such as age or deformity) for expecting parturition to be peculiarly dangerous in the person under examination. Here (except in *primiparæ*) the character of previous labours will, of course, afford valuable aid to our conjectures. In rare instances, however, the Assurance is proposed, if not especially with reference to parturition, at any rate for a limited period of time that is likely to include this event. Here it is usual (and obviously not unfair) to charge a somewhat higher rate to cover the increased risk which the act of childbirth implies, especially where, as a first parturition, it offers greater danger than any subsequent accouchement. Apart from these exceptions, we are bound to remember that all the perils decreed to the female leave her life, as a whole, rather superior to that of the male of corresponding age—in other words, that the pain and danger of childbirth do not bring about an excess of mortality at all approaching that which results from the greater exposure, toil, and intemperance of the stronger sex.

Lastly, it is the combination of the three different kinds of information about which we have been speaking that affords the basis upon which you found your opinion as to the acceptance or rejection of any given proposal. And it is just this, the most difficult part of your duty, respecting which I can give you least assistance. For that basis may either be the sum, or the difference, of many or all of these constituents. In other words, it may be sometimes made up of a variety of favourable or unfavourable circumstances, all tending one way, and therefore leaving you little doubt that it is your duty to accept or reject respectively. But it will more frequently happen that the unfavourable circumstances are so opposed by favourable ones, as to leave you in doubt whether they are not neutralised and practically removed, leaving a clear balance of facts in favour of the proposal.

But even this coarse numerical illustration leaves unnoticed the chief difficulty of such decisions—namely, What degree of stringency are we to use? What is our standard of health; or, conversely, our ground of rejection?

Here again I can only confess my inability to define by words the exact boundary between a Life that we may accept and one that we must decline. Even in practice, such decisions, as difficult as they are important, often tax all that we have of reason and judgment. Indeed, they are frequently based on considerations so many and complex, that we have no right to judge harshly of any conscientious opinion, however much we may personally differ from it.

But it is your duty, I think, to distinguish your report to any Life Office into two kinds of information; which, in every branch of knowledge, it should always be our endeavour to keep apart from each other—matters of opinion, and matters of fact. In respect to the first, we are all liable to err. In respect to the second, there is (or ought to be) a tolerably strict agreement between the evidence of all persons who possess those senses which are the natural means of acquiring information, educated to the particular inquiry. In other words, as regards the facts elicited by a personal examination, you have no business to err. Reasonable skill and care are almost all that is required of you, to ascertain with moderate accuracy the various circumstances just alluded to. And supposing you have done this, I do not say that your opinion is immaterial, but I do say that one of the chief and most important parts of your duty to the Office that employs you is fulfilled.

I am the more anxious to be explicit on this head, because it is one on which great misapprehension seems to prevail amongst the local Medical Referees of Assurance Societies. They occasionally appear to forget that something more than an opinion is wanted of them; that (at least, in many Offices) the facts on which they found that opinion are regarded as equally important; that, in short, their opinion is generally reviewed by a Board of Directors, as well as by another medical referee, whose decision is greatly aided by a knowledge of the same circumstances that have been necessary to form their own.

Hence I will take the liberty of advising you to return answers to *all* the questions transmitted to you, except where they are evidently unanswerable and absurd. It is a great convenience, even as regards the memory, to have a definite form prescribed to you. It is sometimes a still greater advantage to be able to assure an irritable subject of examination that your proceeding (far from being peculiar to him or to yourself) is a routine which you have no choice but to accede to; and that any question which he may be disposed to resent as impertinent is so pertinent, as to form a specific part of your printed instructions. And, finally, I think it becomes our profession to show that it really has a broad and common basis of diagnostic skill :—a catholicity which the various discordant systems of quackery can never lay claim to :—a code of signals respecting disease and health which none but the educated practitioner can appreciate; and which, therefore, it is no way derogatory to him to repeat, as well as to interpret.

I append to these brief allusions a Form of Examination which, in the absence of any prescribed list of questions, you may perhaps find it useful to adopt. Without venturing to regard it as perfect, I think you will find that it so far includes most of the topics we have had to advert to, as to give little chance of anything really important remaining unknown to you, supposing its various questions are propounded with skill on the part of the examiner, and answered with good faith on that of the subject of inquiry.

APPENDIX.

DATE. Name, profession, residence of the person examined.

Apparent age, bodily activity.

Temperance, past and present: nature and amount of alcoholic liquid usually taken.

Father, mother, brothers, and sisters: if living, what age; if dead, cause of death, age at death, respectively.

Any instances of consumption or insanity amongst the above relatives, the uncles, aunts, grandfathers, or grandmothers.

If ever attended medically. Specify the date, duration, and character of maladies hitherto experienced.*

Aspect, complexion, habit of body. Weight (in ordinary dress).

Shape of the chest: its movements in breathing: vital capacity.

Frequency of the respiratory and cardiac sounds. Character as ascertained by auscultation.

State of the pulse. Appearance of the tongue. Vaccination.

In the female, past and present state of uterine functions: character of confinements, if any.

* The proposal of Assurance usually contains a declaration with reference to certain diseases (hæmoptysis, gouts, fits, hernia, habitual cough, &c.), such as would either specially affect the decision, or guide the inquiry, of the Medical Examiner.

C. & E. LAYTON, PRINTERS, 150, FLEET STREET.

BY THE SAME AUTHOR.

This day published,

ON FOOD AND ITS DIGESTION;
BEING
AN INTRODUCTION TO DIETETICS.

8vo. cloth, with 48 Engravings on Wood, 12s.

ALSO,

THE DISEASES OF THE STOMACH.

8vo. cloth, 10s. 6d.

"Certainly no better guarantee could possibly be given for the faithful discharge of the duties implied in writing such a treatise than the previous career of Dr. Brinton. His book is one everywhere inspired by a spirit of truth. It hardly aims at being brilliant or amusing, but it is everywhere readable; and without tediousness, it is earnest, solid, and instructive. Among the numerous works of late years issued upon gastric pathology, it yields to none in importance; and we feel assured that it will be found to supply a want even in this crowded region of medical literature.—To any one who has arrived, by dint of much reading (or much physicking), at conclusions like these, we recommend Dr. Brinton's book; and especially its final Chapter on Dyspepsia, as an example how much the spirit of truth and soberness can do for a subject which has been tortured into such an immense variety of forms.—It is unnecessary to enlarge here upon the exhaustive and admirable manner in which Dr. Brinton has treated of the Chronic Ulcer, and on Cancer of the Stomach.—The same conscientious care for truth has guided the author through every part of his researches, as is apparent in the ground we have now gone over; and indeed not one sentence or phrase from beginning to end of this work will bear the construction that it was written at random, or without the most serious reflection."—*British and Foreign Medico-Chirurgical Review.*

"Dr. Brinton's Lectures cannot fail to add to the high reputation already attained by the author.—In our notice of his monograph of Ulcer of the Stomach, we gave as a reason for the length to which our remarks had run, that it lessened by one affection 'the wide field for speculation, conjecture, and empiricism,' said by Dr. Abercrombie to be presented by diseases of the stomach; and we have now to tender him our thanks for having performed the same good office for the others."—*Dublin Quarterly Journal of Medical Science.*

"In no separate work published in recent years have we met with so clear and exact a statement of the various maladies to which the stomach is liable, of their pathological peculiarities, and the conditions which determine the treatment in the several cases.—The rare judgment and discrimination which mark the author's disquisitions into the value of symptoms and pathological phenomena, make the treatise a reliable one for the practitioner, and constitute it, in fact, *the* reference work on the subject."—*Medical Circular.*

"As one of our first writers upon the structure, functions, and diseases of the alimentary canal, the author of this treatise has for some time established his reputation.—We have been much pleased with the plain and straightforward remarks on dyspepsia. On the subject of indigestion there is such scope for professional as well as other quackery, that it is peculiarly gratifying to alight upon its discussion conducted with as complete an absence of such foible, as with the presence of scientific rigour. We recommend this work as an honourable addition to the really scientific literature of the day."—*Lancet.*

"These lectures are intended to give a brief but complete account of what is at present known concerning the Diseases of the Stomach. To the investigation of these maladies Dr. Brinton has devoted a large amount of time and attention. The whole work will fully repay a careful study; and we therefore heartily commend it to our readers."—*Medical Times and Gazette.*

"Dr. Brinton comes forward with highly favourable antecedents as an observer of, and writer on, Diseases of the Stomach, and the work now before us will increase his well-earned reputation. He has made himself a claim to be looked to as an authority in the subject on which he professes to instruct. Dr. Brinton is an accomplished pathologist in stomach diseases; but, what is of equal, or rather of greater importance, he is manifestly a sound rational therapeutist. What remedies he employs, he employs with judgment, and with a full sense of the difficulties which obstruct his efforts; and, what is of the highest importance, there runs through his therapeutic doctrines an indication to base treatment, as strictly as possible, on physiology. This characteristic of his practice constitutes an additional claim on his part to our confidence."—*Association Journal.*

JOURNAL OF THE INSTITUTE OF ACTUARIES,
AND
ASSURANCE MAGAZINE.

Quarterly, price 2s.

CONTENTS OF VOLUME IX.

No.
39.—New Method for Calculating the Value of an Assurance to the Survivor nominated, &c.—On some Considerations suggested by the Annual Reports of the Registrar-General, being an Inquiry into the question as to how far the inordinate Mortality in this country, exhibited by those Reports, is controllable by human agency (Part I.)—The Life Assurance Companies of Germany: their Business and Position in the Year 1858—Notices of New Works—Institute of Actuaries.

40.—On the Rates of Interest for the Use of Money in Ancient and Modern Times (Part IV.)—On an unfair suppression of due acknowledgment to the writings of Mr. Benjamin Gompertz—On some Considerations suggested by the Annual Reports of the Registrar-General, being an Inquiry into the question as to how far the inordinate Mortality in this country, exhibited by those Reports, is controllable by human agency (Part II.)—Correspondence—Institute of Actuaries.

41.—On the Construction of Life Tables, illustrated by a new Life Table of the Healthy Districts of England—On the Clearing of the London Bankers—On some Considerations suggested by the Annual Reports of the Registrar-General, being an Inquiry into the question as to how far the inordinate Mortality in this country, exhibited by those Reports, is controllable by human agency (Part II.)—On the Composition for Leave to an Assured to reside Abroad—On the Discovery of the Law of Human Mortality, and on the antecedent partial Discoveries of Dr. Price and Mr. Gompertz.

42.—Newton's Table of Leases—On the Construction of Life Tables, illustrated by a new Life Table of the Healthy Districts of England—On Gompertz's Law of Mortality—On the Stability of Results based upon Average Calculations, considered with reference to the Number of Transactions embraced—The American Life Underwriters' Convention—Correspondence.

43.—On the Rates of Premium required to provide certain Periodical Returns to the Assured—Of Compound Interest—Sixth Annual Report of the Insurance Commissioners of the Commonwealth of Massachusetts—Correspondence—Institute of Actuaries.

44.—On the Rate of Mortality prevailing amongst the Families of the Peerage during the 19th century—On the Law of Human Mortality, and on Mr. Gompertz's new exposition of his Law of Mortality—On the various Methods pursued in the Distribution of Surplus among the Assured in a Life Assurance Company; with a comparison of the relative merits of such methods—Correspondence—Institute of Actuaries.

LONDON: CHARLES & EDWIN LAYTON,
150, FLEET STREET, E.C.

DEPOT FOR BOOKS ON ASSURANCE—LIFE, FIRE, AND MARINE.

WORKS
ON
ASSURANCE (LIFE, FIRE, & MARINE), ANNUITIES, FRIENDLY AND BUILDING SOCIETIES, &c.

PUBLISHED OR SOLD BY

CHARLES & EDWIN LAYTON,

Booksellers, Publishers, and Printers,

150, FLEET STREET, LONDON.

DEPOT FOR BOOKS ON ASSURANCE — LIFE, FIRE, & MARINE.

ASSURANCE MAGAZINE, AND JOURNAL OF THE INSTITUTE OF ACTUARIES.
Vols. I. to V., cloth boards, 11s. 6d. each. Vols. VI. to VIII., 13s. 6d. each. Vol. X., Part I., October 1, 1861, 2s.

CHARLES ANSELL, F.R.S.
A TREATISE ON FRIENDLY SOCIETIES;
in which the Doctrine of the Interest of Money, and the Doctrine of Probability, are practically applied to the Affairs of such Societies; with numerous Tables and an Appendix. 8vo. cloth, 5s.

GEORGE ATKINSON.
SHIPPING LAWS OF THE BRITISH EMPIRE;
consisting of PARK on Marine Insurance, and ABBOTT on Shipping. 8vo. cloth, 10s. 6d.

DEPOT FOR BOOKS ON ASSURANCE — LIFE, FIRE, & MARINE.

CHARLES AND EDWIN LAYTON'S LIST OF BOOKS.

CHARLES BABBAGE, M.A., F.R.S.

TABLES OF LOGARITHMS; 1 to 108·000. 8vo. Scarce. On tinted paper.

FRANCIS BAILY.

I.
DOCTRINE OF LIFE ANNUITIES & ASSURANCES, Analytically Investigated and Practically Explained; together with Tables and Appendix. Original Edition. Scarce. 2 vols. 8vo., bound half-calf.

II.
DOCTRINE OF INTEREST AND ANNUITIES, Analytically Investigated and Explained; together with useful Tables. 4to.

III.
TABLES FOR THE PURCHASING AND RENEWING LEASES, for Terms of Years Certain and for Lives.

WILLIAM BRINTON, M.D.

ON THE MEDICAL SELECTION OF LIVES FOR ASSURANCE. Third Edition. 12mo. cloth, 2s.

CHARLES JOHN BUNYON, M.A.

A TREATISE UPON THE LAW OF LIFE ASSURANCE: upon the Constitution of Assurance Companies, the Construction of their Deeds of Settlement, the Sale of Reversionary Interests, and Equitable Liens arising in connection with Life Policies. With an Appendix of Precedents for the Assignment of Policies by way of Sale, Mortgage, and Settlement; Notes of Cases, Statutes, and an Index of Private Acts obtained by Insurance Companies. 8vo. cloth bds., £1. 1s.

DEPOT FOR BOOKS ON ASSURANCE—LIFE, FIRE, & MARINE.

DAVID CHISHOLM.

COMMUTATION TABLES; for Joint Annuities and Survivorship Assurances, for every Combination of Two Lives, according to Carlisle Mortality, at 3, 3½, 4, 5, and 6 per Cent. Interest; with Tables of Annuities and Assurances on Single Lives, and other useful Tables. 2 vols. super royal 8vo. £4. 4s.

FRANCIS CORBAUX.

I.
THE DOCTRINE OF COMPOUND INTEREST; Illustrated and applied to Perpetual Annuities, to those for Terms of Years Certain, to Life Annuities, and generally to Prospective Transactions; with New and Compendious Tables. Imperial 8vo. boards.

II.
TABLES SOLVING THE QUESTIONS THAT DEPEND ON COMPOUND INTEREST, accruing either Annually, Half-Yearly, or Quarterly. Imperial 8vo. boards, 15s.

III.
ON THE NATURAL AND MATHEMATICAL LAWS CONCERNING POPULATION, VITALITY, AND MORTALITY; with Tables of Mortality applicable to Five Classes of each Sex. Imperial 8vo. boards.

GRIFFITH DAVIES, F.R.S.,
ACTUARY TO THE GUARDIAN ASSURANCE COMPANY, AND TO THE REVERSIONARY INTEREST SOCIETY.

TREATISE ON ANNUITIES, with numerous Tables based on the Experience of the Equitable Society and on the Northampton Rate of Mortality. Demy 8vo. boards, £1. 6s.

"The principal feature of this work is the rate of mortality it contains, based upon the experience of the Equitable Society for a period of fifty-seven years, from 1768 to 1825."—*Preface.*

"The construction of Tables, by which deferred, temporary, and increasing benefits are as easily calculated as those for the whole life, belongs to Mr. Barrett; the invention and construction of logarithms to Napier. Mr. Griffith Davies, by various alterations and the separate exhibition of Columns M and R, has increased the utility and extended the power of the method to an extent of which its inventor had not the least idea."—*Professor De Morgan.*

OLINTHUS G. DOWNES, F.R.A.S.

I.
TRANSLATION OF QUETELET'S LETTERS ON THE THEORY OF PROBABILITIES, as applied to the Moral and Political Sciences. 8vo. cloth, 12s.

II.
ON THE PHYSICAL CONSTITUTION OF COMETS. 4to. 6s.

PHILIP A. EAGLE.

LIFE ASSURANCE MANUAL, containing the Principles of Assurance, Life Contingencies, &c. 8vo. cloth, 5s. 6d.

PETER GRAY, F.R.A.S.

TABLES AND FORMULÆ FOR THE COMPU-TATION OF LIFE CONTINGENCIES. 8vo. cloth, 15s.

W. E. HILLMAN.

TABLES OF THE VALUE OF A POLICY OF INSURANCE for £1, according to the Mortality indicated by the Carlisle Observations and also the combined Experience of Life Assurance Companies, at 3, 3½, and 4 per Cent. Interest; with Preparatory Tables for ascertaining the Value of such Insurance for every Age from 14 to 60 Years, and of Duration from 1 to 50 Years. 8vo., bound, £1. 11s. 6d.

WILLIAM INWOOD.

TABLES FOR PURCHASING OF ESTATES (Freehold, Copyhold, or Leasehold), ANNUITIES, ADVOWSONS, &c., and for the Renewal of Leases. 12mo. boards, 7s.

DAVID JONES.
ON THE VALUE OF ANNUITIES & REVERSIONARY PAYMENTS. 2 vols. 8vo. cloth, £1. 10s.

E. & C. H. JONES.
DEBENTURE TABLES; showing the Market Value of Debentures issued at from 4, 5, and 6 per Cent., Terminable in from 1 to 7 Years. Post 8vo., half-calf, £1. 10s.

WILLIAM LANCE.
ON MARINE INSURANCE. 8vo. cloth, 3s.

S. L. LAUNDY.
TABLE OF QUARTER-SQUARES OF ALL INTEGER NUMBERS up to 100,000, by which the Product of Two Factors may be found by the aid of Addition and Subtraction alone. Royal 8vo., 21s.

J. MARSHALL.
TABLES AND TRACTS connected with the Valuation, whether of Annuities and Assurances contingent on the Duration of Life, or of Sums and Annuities Certain; with various Formulæ and Incidental Notices. Fcap. folio, 7s. 6d.

JOSHUA MILNE.
TREATISE ON ANNUITIES. 2 vols. 8vo. boards. Very scarce.

CHARLES AND EDWIN LAYTON'S LIST OF BOOKS.

F. G. P. NEISON, F.L.S.

VITAL STATISTICS: being a Development of the Rates of Mortality and Laws of Sickness; with an Inquiry into the Influence of Locality, Occupations, and Habits of Life, on Health, &c. &c. Third Edition. 4to., £2. 2s.

WILLIAM ORCHARD.

ON ASSURANCE PREMIUMS, Single and Annual; with Preliminary Treatise by PETER GRAY, F.R.A.S. 8vo. cloth, 10s. 6d.

WYATT PAPWORTH.

I.

NOTES ON CAUSES OF FIRES; or, which is the Safest of various Methods of Warming Buildings. 1s. 6d.

II.

NOTES ON SPONTANEOUS COMBUSTION. 1s.

T. G. RANCE.

TABLES OF COMPOUND INTEREST, for every Quarter, from ¼ to 10 per Cent., and for every Year from 1 to 100 Years. Royal 8vo. cl., £1. 1s.

EDWARD SANG, F.R.S.E.

I.

LIFE ASSURANCE AND ANNUITY TABLES. Folio, cloth lettered. Vol. I. (One Life), £4. 4s. Ditto, Vol. II. (Two Lives), £4. 4s. Now ready. Or the Two Vols., £7. 7s.

II.

ESSAY ON LIFE ASSURANCE. 5s.

DEPOT FOR BOOKS ON ASSURANCE—LIFE, FIRE, & MARINE.

CHARLES AND EDWIN LAYTON'S LIST OF BOOKS.

A. SCRATCHLEY, M.A., F.R.A.S.,
FORMERLY FELLOW AND SADLERIAN LECTURER OF QUEEN'S COLLEGE, CAMBRIDGE.

I.
TREATISE ON LIFE ASSURANCE SOCIETIES
AND FRIENDLY SOCIETIES; with an Exposition of the True Law of Sickness, the Mathematical Principles for Valuing the Affairs of Life Offices for *Bonus Divisions or Amalgamations*, and the Theory of Assurance and Annuities. 8vo. boards. Tenth Edition. 7s. 6d.

II.
INDUSTRIAL INVESTMENT & EMIGRATION:
being a Treatise on Benefit Building Societies and Tontines, and on the General Principles of Associations for Land Investment and Colonization; with some New Theorems in the Doctrine of Compound Interest. Third Edition. 8vo. boards, 7s. 6d.

III.
TREATISE ON LIFE ASSURANCE SOCIETIES
AND FRIENDLY SOCIETIES, AND INDUSTRIAL INVESTMENTS AND EMIGRATION. Together, forming 1 volume, cloth, 15s.

IV.
TREATISE ON THE ENFRANCHISEMENT OF
COPYHOLD, LIFE-LEASEHOLD, AND CHURCH PROPERTY; with Tables for the Purchasing and Renewing of Leasehold Estates, and for Advowsons and Next Presentations. Fourth Edition. 12mo. boards, 3s. 6d.

V.
FORMULÆ FOR THE VALUATION OF POST
OBITS AND CONTINGENT REVERSIONS, OR LEGACIES. New Edition. 8vo., 1s.

VI.
TREATISE ON SAVINGS BANKS. New Edition;
with Rules, Tables, and numerous Statistics. 8vo. boards, 14s.

B. H. TODD.
LIFE ASSURANCE INVESTIGATION TABLES;
showing the Value of £100 Policy for any Number of Years not exceeding Fifty, according to Carlisle 3 per Cent. 8vo. cloth, £1. 1s.

DEPOT FOR BOOKS ON ASSURANCE—LIFE, FIRE, & MARINE.

W. T. THOMSON, F.R.S.E.

I.
ACTUARIAL TABLES: Carlisle 3 per Cent., Single Lives, and Single Death; with Auxiliary Tables. 4to. cloth, £2. 2s.

II.
LENDERS AND BORROWERS ON LANDED SECURITIES. 1s.

R. A. WARD.

TREATISE ON INVESTMENTS: being a Popular Exposition of the Advantages and Disadvantages of each kind of Investment, and the Liability of it to Depreciation and Loss. 8vo. cloth. Second Edition, enlarged. 10s. 6d.

CHARLES M. WILLICH.

I.
POPULAR TABLES: arranged in a New Form, giving Information at Sight, for ascertaining, according to the Carlisle Table of Mortality, the Value of Lifehold, Leasehold, and Church Property, Renewal Fines, &c.; also various Interesting and Useful Tables, equally adapted to the Office and the Library Table. Fourth Edition. 12mo. cloth, 10s.

II.
INTEREST & TITHE COMMUTATION TABLES, from 2¼ to 10 per Cent., 2s.

WILLIAM WOOD.

CONVERSION TABLES. Foolscap folio, sewed, 5s.; cloth, 7s. 6d.

DEPOT FOR BOOKS ON ASSURANCE—LIFE, FIRE, & MARINE.

www.ingramcontent.com/pod-product-compliance
Lightning Source LLC
Chambersburg PA
CBHW032245080426
42735CB00008B/1017